"Simply Me"

"Simply Me"

PRIVATE MOMENTS FOR A PUBLIC HEALING

Lisa Barber

authorHOUSE®

AuthorHouse™ LLC
1663 Liberty Drive
Bloomington, IN 47403
www.authorhouse.com
Phone: 1-800-839-8640

Published by AuthorHouse   01/17/2014

ISBN: 978-1-4918-4929-3 (sc)
ISBN: 978-1-4918-4930-9 (e)

Library of Congress Control Number: 2014900179

Dedications

This book dedication goes to my father,
Joseph William Barber Sr. a man
who will be remembered by his dialog of rhyming phrases
that left behind many smiles.

Also to Ashley Barber,
my niece of 22 years, who did not
get the chance to reveal the hidden treasures of
poetry God gifted her with during the trials of her heart.

Last, but never the least dedication belongs
to my God, Lord and Savior, who allowed
life to form off the pages of "SIMPLY ME"
from the inspiration of His Word

Contents

"The Private"

"The Prayer"

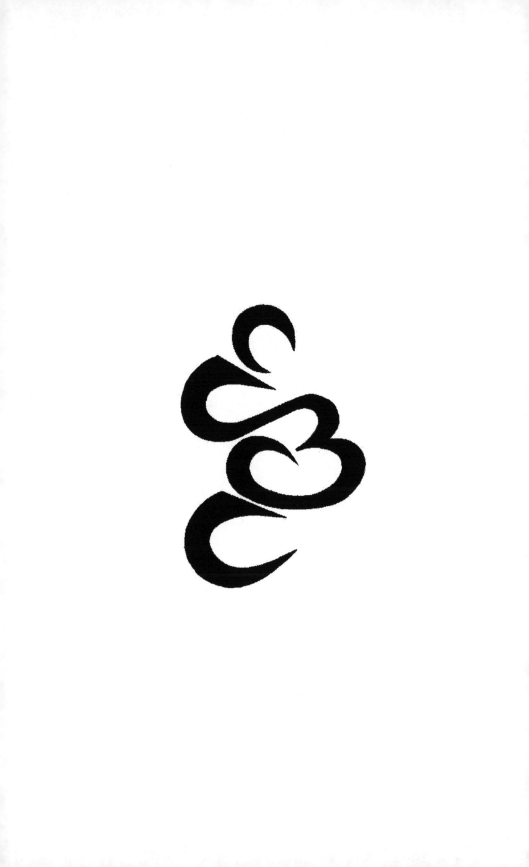

"Simply Me"

Change we need
Nation is hunger
Time to feed
nutrients of love
Pain so great
can't see above
Transform minds
Skin don't matter
truth becomes all kinds
Emotion defeat
War so long
brain is beat
Positive over negative
Like your enemy
take a place to live
Pride dominate
Nothing else you know
breathe in hate
Listen up
observe the signs
Things so corrupt
Sensitive ear
begin the process
the Word to hear

Action to do
wake up
Have you no clue?
Small feet don't know
Wise bones
explain and show
Encourage all
great to come
No time to fall
Excusable if you do
battle still there
until you get through
Know the purpose!
Go after
Refuse to fuss
Right in the heart
Covered up
Refocus and start
Begin to see
the ability
for unity
and liberty
Winning the victory
Is just simply me

Acknowledgements

I have to give thanks to my four children,
Andre, Erica, Jovon and Carl
For your moments
shared with me. The moments I experience
for myself and those moments
I could only imagine you going through. You
have help me to develop a rock
to stand on during your trying times.
I applaud my best friend, Etoil Anderson for her encouragement,
motivation and just keeping it real
I want to thank the many others, friends and family that became
an inspiration to my writing, as well.
I especially give thanks to God who gives me the creative ability
to write and speak in a poetic way.

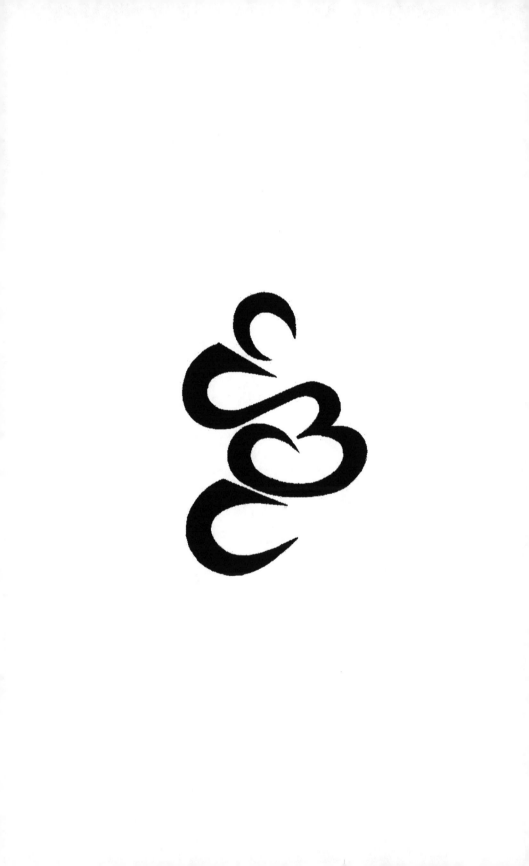

"The Push"

Who's in the way?

Pardon me, excuse me!
You're in the way
Blinded by your views
on how to start my day
Shut up! Stop talking!
I need to hear
my agenda made clear
Who are you
to tell me what to do?
Controlling my life
talking about what, when & who
Muddle in my ear
I have to confess
Clouding my decisions
never at rest
You're the reason
for this discomfort, this pain
Confusion every 5 minutes
no win to gain
So I'm in lack . . . .
wanting me to settle
Shout outs from the unwise
they just want to meddle
Constantly imitating
my screw ups . . . come on now
relieve, I'm waiting
No more drama
No more drama
Just because of sin
I was born in
from the wound
of my momma

Deceitful plans
become successful
The blurry road
got me headed for trouble
I'm going through
and bad advise you give me more
Walking in some one else affliction
has my heart soar
I knew I should have
got up before you
To seek some other advise
that would take me through
I should have got down on my knees
until no temptation in me
would dare to be tease
I should have read Psalms 23
for my security
Why did I first come to you
I should have let you be
Because that person in the way
that person is me

Had To Be

I had a dream, so excite about
decided to plan, bring it on out
Drew out a timeline, three years it would take
Had to be serious
buckle down and concentrate
Not realizing the set up for opportunity
creativity and productivity
to help others develop
Had to be discipline
if this dream I had would surface to win
Some things I would not be able to do
Had to be strong
had to get through
And those party friends, always a tease
couldn't give in though
Had to be determined
even if they said "please"
Cause this dream I had
spectators was waiting to see
Did I have what it take
or was I gone let this dream be?
There were days my dream tried to fade away
Had to be motivated
start fresh another day
The challenge was hard
so was finding my sources
Had to be knowledgeable, make the right choices
My time was near to bring this dream about
Had to be focus, ignore family
looking me up and down in doubt
I felt pressured, a little uneasy too

Had to be obedient
go back to what I knew how to do
I had to remember the One
seek out the One, and trust the One
Who put this dream in me
the One who already set the destiny
Who told me this dream "had to be"
So without hesitation, I continued the race
Had to be diligent
make sure things were in place
I added, subtracted to my daily routine
Had to be consistent
if I was to share the blessings
And because there were many before
who walked such a journey
Had to be inspired, cause this dream
I had was not for me

The Ingredients

There I was
opened like a mixing
bowl waiting to be filled
My character was ready
to be worked on
my insides anxious to be build
I began to acknowledge
all I didn't have
I gather all I would need
One by one
I would get it in, I believe
a good thing never has to speed
LOVE was first going in
with all my might
I was careful about getting this right
Next, blend in my JOY you see
cause life issues
always tried to take it from me
Slowly, I had to stir in PEACE
cause no matter what the battle
it would soon seize
Didn't take a liking
to the LONGSUFFING
but it was well needed too
In order to deal with life's issues
in order to get through
Now GENTLENESS &
GOODNESS
could be stirred in together
complimenting flavors I need forever
I thought I had my FAITH
when I first got started

I need it always
so I won't be broken-hearted
Last, MEEKNESS &
TEMPERANCE
sprinkle on delicately
Life's wear downs and tear downs
Pushes me drastically
But the heat applied
will always release
a sweet-smelling nature
from the aroma of a strong character

What is this I
den stepped into?

I wake up to my cell phone
cause you got to know my mind
Releasing my bitter, my anger, my hate
soothes me all the time
Now that I've set your day with my agenda
Got to style for the world
don't care if I offend ya!
My mentality makes me think I'm what's up
My position, it's rude, it's nasty
it's naughty, doing right just never develop
Ghetto . . . fab..u..lous, yeah, that's me
My loudness covers up my insecurity
Twice I walk the hood, styling in my video fit
cause I'm looking good
Got to make sure they see me
dare someone to say something
Oh I wish they would
Now I'm playing Deebo, Devon & lil Dee
gangsters, if you will
as long as the tables don't turn
and they have me trick'n for a meal
But I'll do it, cause that's the only love I know
Momma working overtime, all the time
and daddy . . . well, no show
And nine months later
look what all that kind of love got me
Another life to care for
now what can I show them
When I can't even see . . . .

That there is a God
who will forgive my sins
all I have to do is repent and don't do it again
That there is a life I can live abundantly
that I can do all things great
Through a God who will strengthen me
That I can become
the head and not the tail
That there is a God
to build my confidence so I won't fail
Because there is a God
who loves me and shows me favor
I can show the same
kind of love for my neighbor
That there really
is a place I can go to, a place of rescue
Oh what is this I den stepped into

This Is What I Say

Don't neglect your future
avoid your dreams or
resist the promises given to you
Don't let them abort it
you've got to
prepare the way
Cause this is what I say
Don't procrastinate
think you got time or
"oh I'll get to it" . . . . do it!
It's your vision, plain
and clear, to put before man
So get to it, don't delay
Cause this is what I say
There is a plan for your life
a purpose just for you
Go forward with confidence
Be strong and
courageous
as you move on your way
Cause this is what I say
Remember to be determined
Know who you are
You might have to
stand still and wait
Patience will become you
as you seek my
presence everyday
I will speak to you
"this is what I say"

When you look at me

When you look at me, don't look at my past
Looking down on me, the bad things I did last
Don't look at what I was, when you look at me
Can you get pass my past
of the old me I use to be
Stop judging me, keeping up with my failed test
I'm just like you, a work in progress
So I'm going to keep telling myself
I'm brand new until I become brand new
and do what I suppose to do
When you look at me
don't think you know my thoughts
Never consider who I am now
Cause you holding on to all my faults
My past is my past no matter how long ago
Can you stop going in on me
just let the negative go
When you look at me, focus on my good deeds
Motivate me to accomplish
more of those needs
Do it hurt so much when you look at me
You see yourself so you get angry
Vision a redeemed want to be
As I work on the new, improved me
Cause when you look at me
You will see old things passed away
The day will come when you will have
Nothing negative left to say

I have given up

I have given up
who I thought I was
walking around in this world
trying to be of this world
just because
I have given up
trying to be apart
of the clique
so I can think
that I'm liked
by certain people . . . .
no . . . . that ain't it
I have given up
my insecurities
on what to wear
how to style my hair
Now I'm bold and
confident in doing me
I don't care if they stare
I have given up
the idea of being lonely
I will stand alone
for as long to be
Man will have to be made whole
if he want to get with me
I have given up
being afraid
of anything or anybody
I can do all things
cause the spirit of fear
doesn't dwell in me
I have given up

habits me body should not bare
So I pay close attention
what I let enter
This is my temple
and for that I do care
I have given up
the negatives of my mind
thinking and living
a positive life
happiness I will find
I have given up
thinking I'm the one in control
you see . . . .
my life doesn't belong to me
a price was paid
to save my soul

If we knew

If we knew what love
you have for us
would learning to love
be a must
If we knew our debt
was too great to face
we'd be grateful you stepped in
to take our place
If we knew how blessed
we are, would we know
you will never go away too far
If we knew you was just a call away
would we let you in our every day
If we knew how to learn
and control our flesh
we wouldn't be deceived by all the plans
against us being accomplish
If we knew the real deal
behind being saved
we'd let our light shine
by the way we behave
If we knew how quick you forgive
we'd stop trying to put people
in hell base on how they live
If we knew the significance
in your blood
we'd stop letting the enemy punk us
when he pours in like a flood
If we knew our lives
are not lived on emotion
our state of being
may be free of extra commotion

If we knew to pray and intercede
for other on what they do
maybe we'd realize
it's how you live your life
that judges you
If we knew the day
when "this " would all come to a fold
I wonder . . . .
would humanity be so cold

My brother

Thought I was living
life the best I could
But my brother I married
kept me in the hood
I was easy, he was cheesy
He couldn't free me
This lifestyle I grew up in
Inside and outside
watching sin
Everyday stares
made my life condition
My ears plugged
made no transition
I was immune, he was in tune
With all the sin
in the hood
Body would soon
be no good
Took no more. I wanted out!
This brother I married
had no clout
Being in the world
made him blend
Never taste good
at the end
I decided to divorce
right away
from a stagnant life
every single day
Sound in my ear

I could begin to hear
my transition
was finally near
mind speaking
to the brother
with the same intend
for many others

Battle down

Battle down
what crushes you
Beware what rushes you
How many "this is it"
you willing to face
before you get snatch
from this place
Battle down
what forces you
Beware of yourself
because, of course its you
Trying to decide when
"this is absolutely it"
So in a confuse place
you just sit
Your freedom is crowding in
wondering if you're going
to take your turn to win
Battle down
what rejects you
Beware of what
injects you
Remember the good times
places the smile
determination will help
you remember how
Don't layer your pain
feeling sluggish
Reflecting back
On broken rubbish

Battle down
negativity
Beware of captivity
That smothers
and uses others
to drain out of you
life that should be lived
In abundances
But "this is it"
is still at a distance
Battle down
condemnation
Beware of foolish
persuasion
don't waste time
keeping up strife
You got to battle down
Stop living useless life

I do what I do

The things that I do
are the things I shouldn't
The things I should do
are the things I wouldn't
"that" that I do
not by spirit but by flesh
knocks me to my feet
in distress
Deceiving myself
to do what I do
Don't think
what I do to me or you
Consequences
are never in demand
I do what I do
all because I can
Now how can I do
that what I shouldn't
against the Creator
who let's me choose
those things I wouldn't
Satan has twisted hearts
with this lie, many soul
don't care what happen
to them once they die

"The Purpose"

Who knows it?

Love is expression
with no fear
of my impression
My soul says be creative
cause that's how
I was born to live
I am voice
I have choice
Is my right your wrong
or my wrong your right?
Whose to say
whose to make that call?
Isn't life full of lessons
for us all
Should my heart
be open to receive
if you know
what it's like
so I won't grieve
Any, many, mighty, more
most of us find
the answer after
our minds
get plenty sore
Challenged
with lessons everyday
Is it worth it
falling repeatedly
until I learn to love
the right way
Tired of my flesh
wrestling with my spirit

My peace is near
and I know it
To love
with no limitation
My body can linger
in relaxation
Knowing what's with me
knowing what's in me
knowing what's for me
Now my love
can be made easy

This is the day

This is the day
you showed me love
Now I can come
outside of me
Share my loving beauty
This is the day
you showed me favor
Now I can put away
selfish expectation
Show pleasing invitations
This is the day
you gave me peace
Now I can be wise
what I say, so
"we both "will be able
to walk away
This is the day
you gave me hope
Now I can breathe
without worry
things I can't fix
on my own ability
This is the day
you gave me strength
Now even in my worse day
deep down I can
make it anyway
This is the day
you made me smile
Now I can bring
on some laughter

exploring my
sense of humor
This is the day
you made for me
Now I can rejoice
I can be glad
for the blessings
I never knew I had

A good day

I'm on my way
to say what I need to say
To start a new day
Cause today is a good day
I'm glad I opened my eyes
Did no cheating
stealing and no lies
I can receive my prize
The things that belong to me
it's no surprise
Cause today is a good day
I'm different to do
what I need to do
Share with you and you
humor your soul if I have to
Cause today is a good day
I have the opportunity
to see the sun
Even if I'm going through
I can still enjoy the fun
And in my heart
I can feel a smile
since it's my race
I've already won
Cause today is a good day
I can excuse your "my bad"
Have nothing to prove
don't have to get mad
over angry words
that was said
Cause today is a good day

Let me rub on you
so I can rub off on you
and to someone else
you too
and on and on
and on and you
can be an unusual "who"
Cause today is a good day

I'm that one

I can be your friend, I'm that one if you let me try
I'll be there for you and you be there for me
You can choose you and I
You can pick my mind cause I'll motivate you
Never worry about distrusting me
I'm there when you go through
Think of me when you look up at the stars
Never will be hard to find
I'll always know exactly where you are
When you going through test
I'll give you what you need
to make sure you do your best
I'm that one to give you a hand
if you're in lack
I'll do more for you than you think I can
Angry and upset, I can help you get over that too
Can't control your temper, want to get violent
Let me show you what to do
I'm that one that you can take from good advice
Listen to me don't get double-mined
start thinking twice
If you're a little fearful that's okay
Cause by the time I get through with you
You'll be well on your way
Walking in confidence, no time for getting mad
cause you trusted in me to bring out those things
in you I always knew you had
But be humble
Don't think you do what you do
Your mind is not that great to think things through
So give me a shout out
with praises from your gestures, of course

Could be left to yourself making the wrong choice
But I'm that one who will never leave you
I'm that one that will let your tribulations make you
Don't be afraid when they come
singing a new tune is where
the beat will sound from
I'm that one you should talk to first
Guaranteed to lay on your mind
more to quench your thirst
And you can begin to live life and not die
Because you will want to do what it takes
instead of just getting by
Begin to see the doors open, peace will unfold
Opportunity will roll right on in and life
you will spend, in this world
that has already taken you on a delusional
manipulating, crazy swirl
See the doors open greatness is waiting
forget about those hating
You will be there to share, which could only be fair
To place the joy in those that only could bare
I'm that one that can do "that" thing
help you to a epic lifestyle
That 's what I choose to bring

Let's stop playing

We made another year
So let's get it straight
it's time to receive
all things great
God has it for us
cause with Him we need
an open ear
to put our trust
He's the truth
He's the light
It's by His grace and mercy
We even wake up
So lets make it right
Let's find out
what God has already said
through His Word
Stop playing
let's get to know Him
for our self
not just from what we've heard
We must seek Him first
Early on a daily
Develop a thirst
To love Him
fear Him, trust Him
With our whole heart
Steadfast
and never part
Focus and concentrate
Begin every year to celebrate
cause he has an agenda
for His people

Let's stop playing
let's get full
of His knowledge
understanding, and wisdom
Let's turn our lives around
And give Him some love
In His kingdom

Changed mind

Where can you go
without a changed mind
You're stuck, eyelid shut
you're walking blind
You're comfortable
or hopeless
in a world
of unnecessary mess
very unnecessary
Made choices
to big for you to carry
Your many days
are bitter and mad
Only blackness
finds your tears
when you are sad
Your finger scatter
to every voice
that knows you
Instead of coming back home
to face what is true
You can't think about
a changed mind
until you establish
the willingness to find
A happier way to live
If you can find in your heart to give
up the control
you thought you had
cause really the devil
he's pulling your way

making you that bitter and mad
Yeah, he do exist
so do Jesus
whom I'd rather not resist
You can begin
to have a changed mind
when you seek the Lord
and find the doors
of happiness and love
Peace and joy
all comes from up above
Jesus can show you
what you've been missing
all this time
If you would only
take the first step
and have a changed mind

Change your thoughts

You living out thoughts going nowhere
Wandering around
parties of despair
You choose wrong
then say life's not fair
Maybe you need to change your thoughts
Instagram lifestyle
got you headed deep in dirt
you swallow your heart
to avoid from getting hurt
Listening to the delusions in your mind
Always on the battlefield
concluding life's just fine
Is it possible you need to change your thoughts
You say you strong and follow no one
but your pants below it's purpose
came from someone
Other than you, so let's be true
whose following who
Now your eyes were tried
when Katrina hit New Orleans
and here comes Sister Sandy
You better wake up
from your fantasy dreams
Evil just don't stand a chance
good just isn't good enough
Shouldn't you rethink some things
get on some right kind of stuff
You should want to think the right things
Or do it the right way
Instead of taking someone
out of their day

Taking a son from his mother
a mother from her child
a sister from her brother
Cause crazy thoughts
got you running wild
And all because you simply
don't know how
to change your thoughts
It's a process, I'm hear to suggest
you digest
to keep you from meditating
on senseless mess
Change your thoughts

Can't I just

Doing the thing I do just to get the luxury
Pant down to my knee
Why can't I just discover me?
Can't think of being lonely
Evil just won't flee
Flesh so doggone needy
Can't I just be free
Been kept from the county
And from death especially
Because of acts of stupidity
Hoping for grace and mercy
Blame always on the community
Wrong has me as property
Not right with my destiny
Why can't I just say no to the enemy?
Body struggling mentally
Of bad childhood memory
Always was found guilty
Just never could be sorry
But now seeking advice early
Requesting some things specifically
Doing some things courageously
Why can't I just engage in unity?
To the world I got to be stingy
God yes! I say, not maybe
For my soul I would have eternity
Why can't I just live
for the One, Great and Mighty

Expecting Blessing Everyday

Think you untouchables
Cause you're not afraid to die
Life is more than what you're living
Escaping the drive by
fueding with the you's and I's
Cause you refuse to try
Walk away
don't get buried away
Forget those
who thinks you 're soft
Cause your aim
is always off
Work out your issues
Tired of poster board
senseless miss you's
Settle with one another
Love yourself
then your brother
Take your stand
with other lives at hand
Live like you got plans to stay
Conquer the mind set of
Expecting blessing everyday

MATURITY

M is for making
a change for good
making sure living life
is well understood
A is for asking
about things you don't know
so you'll be closer to your purpose
as it begins to show
T is for turning
away from negativity
engage in productivity
experience longevity
U is for understanding
as you become knowlegable
And never, ever
think you are unteachable
R is for running
this race no matter what
even if you go through
a season you feel stuck
I is for identifying
distractions along the way
as you begin your
adventure everyday
T is for time
you have not to waste
by letting people
trick you out of your
position you're about to face
Y is for yes
yes to change
yes to taking on the challenge

No matter the set backs
Don't let impurity
idolatry
or insecurity
comes to steal
your identity
or rob your destiny
Life happen
as you grow and reach
maturity

EPHESIAN

God has blessed me
with His blessings in the earth
He thought of me
He loved me, from the very
beginning even before my birth
I am chosen by God
to be holy without fault
in His love
how grateful I am
for that Great name above
For only such special
such unique blood
can redeem such a sinful me
And because of His riches
of His merciful grace
forgiveness is all He see
Even though He saw
the disobedient me
running after the desired
of my flesh, and I realized
it was due to my lustful eyes
I am still His workmanship
able to fight against principalities
against powers, rulers of the darkness
spiritual wickedness in high places (Ephesian 6:12)
I am equip
I am filled with God's spirit
not man's wine
So I speak with boldness
about this Great Savior of mine
invite Him in your heart
where He can dwell

Don't forget about others
they need Him as well
Your issues may be easy to resolve
Unlike before when they were
impossible to solve
Sure no magician can zap
anger from you
But it will be very hard to grab
if you're use to picking up a 45', 38' or 22'
God said in His word
be angry but do not sin
"I created your spirit
with the flesh you're in"
It's easy to believe deception
led by our flesh
When decisions are made
from "such like" mind
is all we have left
If we learn Him
we will learn the spirit in us
If we learn Him
we will learn the knowledge in us
If we learn Him
we will learn the love in us
If we learn Him
we will learn the strength in us
Because "now unto us that is able
to do exceedingly, abundantly
above all that we ask or think
according to the power that work in us" (Ephesian 3:20)
As we continue to pray to our
Lord Christ Jesus

The Wind

Where the wind blows far
cool sensations
takes me where you are
The breezy
sets the tone, relaxed
and easy
Drifting pass the wind
in an unknown atmosphere
placing you in my space
right here
How far do the wind blows
There's only One who knows
Imagination
Can you see it?
it's inspiration
To know where the wind
blows far
is motivating
to get me where you are

Praises Over the Storm

The storm confuses
just a bit
Press through
give your best worship
The storm comes
to take you out
Praises will remove
any doubt
Away, the storm
washes the sea
Loud praises
rushes it to flee
The storm strips
the mind to defeat
Continual praises
celebrate the beat
The storm positions
to a low place
Praises show
victories to face
The storm must never
be put before God
cause praises will scatter
your storm abroad

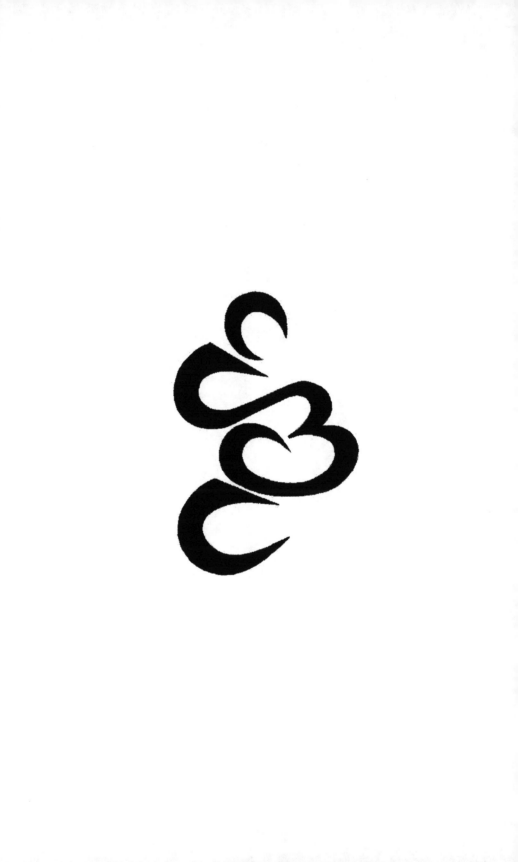

"The Private"

The Gift

It was no surprise
When I saw you
Such a wonderful joy
bringing you home
in something other than blue
It was no mystery
you'd challenge me
You was just what I needed
to bring out who
I am suppose to be
Your restless nights made me
your private vocalist
Soon after you'd drift off
I'd seal your peace with a kiss
As you develop into
your growing years, you see
there's a lot to walk into
to raise your curiosity
As a child it was much easier
to protect you
But now your path is constructed
just to go through
Your struggles made you strong
You showed the world
you can stand alone
And being silly doesn't
take away your character
This world needs to enjoy
the great sound of laughter
So you know the gift
behind a big smile
one you display well

just to show the world how
You collect attention
not just by your beauty alone
By dropping a seed
knowing it will be sown
Your heart was design
for a purpose in mind
Your motion sets out to show
the world how to be kind
And because God has given you
the greatest gift above
you truly know how to share
the gift of Love

My Deliverance

I opened my eyes, blaming life's
up's and down's for putting him here
Fulfilling the world, not my own
did I not care or was it fear
Moments of love into likes
Moments of likes into dislikes
Dislikes into hate
and each and every day
we would create
these scenes over and over again
Until I freed my eyes of deception
knew this was not the end
I came into the spirit of faith
even though I knew I was the one
that made the mistake
Didn't beat myself about it
I just made the transit
Baby boy tried to play hard
But his ego was scarred
I decided to seek the face
of the Lord for strength
To get rid of that thing
no matter where it went
But I ask God to help him as well
cause by himself, on his face
he would surely fail
For me, there were day's
I got through
Believing Jesus was affecting him too
Those days I had to repent
get back up like I was already delivered

praise the Lord and on I went
Determined I wasn't carnal-mined
Struggling to get through
peace I was going to find it
No matter what
I praised Him
glorified His name
I was now confident
in my deliverance to claim

I use to walk without knowing

As a little girl, I saw momma "never being"
who she was suppose to be
And daddy "all the time drinking"
couldn't take care of me
I use to walk without knowing
I was mentally by myself, physically too
My sister and brother out on they're own
Doing what they do
Momma always went away
to get help for being "so special"
Daddy had to go to work
to put food on the table
But old man Ernest
became a familiar face I use to see
True friend of my daddy's
cause he never took advantage of me
I use to walk without knowing
Where was my family? I sure didn't have a clue
There where many days
I was left with people I never even knew
I was often at a place where I didn't like being me
So it didn't take much thought
to create an imaginary family
As a teen, I tried to turn into a troubled child
Drinking, getting high just on the weekend so
I wouldn't become addictively wild
My self conscious was okay
with me being this type of user
Caring what others thought of me
stop me from being an out of control abuser

I use to walk without knowing
I made it to college to study
what I was sure I wanted to be
Can't say I waste five years
cause the major I choose just wasn't in me
By the time I took on my third job
I had two mouths to feed
Had to do what I had to do
with a demand to supply their need
The choices I had already made of destruction
was ordain to build me up on good construction
I walked this road according to plan
my life was in a more trustworthy hand
Not only was I one of the few
that had been called
I was chosen, cause I got back on my feet
every time I would fall
I use to walk without knowing
And little did I know my path
was already known to be to push out who I was
to develop a true character in me
Life episodes continued
to bring heartache and pain
But if I knew it was molding me
in getting closer to my purpose
I probably would not have complain

My Rightful Position

I was raised as an SMO, going to church" Sunday Morning Only
But Monday through Saturday
never came close to the church door
I was told "God do exist"
but where, wasn't quite sure
daddy never invited him over
never heard God's name
come out of his mouth on purpose'
But "the Lord is my shepherd, I shall not want"
was the opening page to our family bible
on my momma's dresser
No one ever turned the page or even asked what
else did God say, no, no one dared
to take on that added pressure
In my household, momma's and daddy's
fighting was practical
so it never led one of them away
just made our family dysfunctional
And the older I got the more confused I became
My routine was to lie to make myself look good
steal to get what I want
then repent in Jesus name
Now because I was in control, life beat me bad
Anger, bitter, jealousy, deceit, fear
and low, low self esteem was what I had
It wasn't until I decided enough was enough
I couldn't do this no more
sick and tire of being sick and tire
The devil was gone give me back my stuff
So I began to let the dust
roll off the pages of Psalms 23
to "the Lord is my light & salvation" . . . went on to

"Plead my cause, O Lord" to "
"Fret not thyself because of evildoers" . . . .
The Lord was building up something in me
I decided to go back to Genesis
to see how God created this world
Very strategic how He made woman for man
Hmm . . . and all this time I thought it was cool
Tina was dating Sheryl
But I realized the Word bring correction to all
cause it checked me too
In Deuteronomy I get a gleams
of some of the rules & regulations
so if I didn't know, now I have a clue
I had consumed a lot of information
Started to feel guilty knowing all I had did
Then I read
"God commended his love towards me
I heard Him whisper, "No Condemnation!
So I made the transition
With conviction I felt the obligation
because of the revelation
to give God my attention
to get in my rightful position
after all, He laid it down just for me
His life, His blood
on the cross, waiting that I may grabbed
life eternity

My flesh

My flesh, was acting bad
Seductively on fire
I gave him the idea
he was someone I was ready to desire
His conversation was all over me
like a baby eating their birthday cake
Oh boy! I knew it
I had made a big mistake
But my nature was enjoying what I was hearing
I had totally forgot
whom I should be fearing
His swag took me there
in our honeymoon suite
just day two
in conversation, on the phone
it was about to go down, once we meet
In his head
I was just a passenger with no intention
of getting to my destination
cause I didn't want to revisit condemnation
My flesh wanted the man
but it couldn't understand
the right way not by what my flesh say
Cause it would sure to do wrong
probably wouldn't even last too long
I can't give it up like that again
off of what . . . two minutes of sin
My flesh had to be denied
of those lustful desired I wasn't shame to hide
Snap back Christian
you know you got the saint listening

and watching you under a microscope
trying to see if you can cope
With the pressures of this world
instead of praying for you, girl
I am more than a conqueror I say
I can fight this flesh any day
no matter how long it takes to see
my flesh will not win and control me

Who Do You Think You Are?

Christian
who do you think you are?
Can't win this battle alone
Need God always
as a child, even when
you think you're grown
Christian
who do you think you are?
You're not doing it
by yourself, never
God shows His hand always
He's here forever
For your strength, health and fame
Watch out!
The devil is waiting to step in, cause
to him your life is just a game
Christian
who do you think you are?
Forgetting to talk to God
about your choices
So high up, strung up
you can't distinguish the voices
to tell you what to do
how to do or when to do it
Dangerously flesh has taken over
but you won't admit
Christian
who do you think you are?
Started out trying to give
Godly advice
Look in the mirror now
Do you still represent Christ?

My Journey

This walk is a journey of design
my special path for me to find
Specific assignments to take on
Figure out what I am made of
from the time I was born
As a child I was very special
thoughts of madness
came to take me out
but He sent me a protecting angel
Many times I would find myself
on my own
Didn't know "not fitting in "
will be apart of walking
this journey alone
Fear came in my teens, rested on my heart
denied me blessings
because I fell to do my part
Often the walk will be dim as dirt
The light may never show itself
until after many times
of getting hurt
Tears will have to role from the eye
so the process of healing can begin
Time can only make it well to say goodbye
I stand strong today taking on this challenge
Can't go back, can't say no
Cause the purpose of my journey
is to finish

I AM FREE

I am free
God let's me be
I'm in His place
to feel His warm embrace
His loving arms
gently around me
I am free
Taking control
of my destiny
His direction
singles out distraction
pressing pass
the media's chatter
Plotting to keep
me from the latter
I am free
to experience
epic expectations
for me
Struggles comes
to give up and don't care
Starting over
begins somewhere
I witness his divine dealing
As he keeps on revealing
His Word
through my experiences
I thank Him
for interferences
I am free
Don't live like I want to be

But as I am as I shine
through the blessings
of mine
Sin comes to interrupt
Quick confessions
cancel the corrupt
I am free
I know I should be
I am strong
Temptation don't linger long
I am free
because of what He gave
on Calvary
Through my motions I live
keeping my love for Him active
Praying in His name
I proclaim
Jesus came
I am free

A Complete Finish

Total blank, no words
see no image, nothing express
Only anxiously waiting my touch to confess
One stroke, two stroke, phenomenal
Flat back, laid back, diagonal
Color bound left to right
holds the composure sealed tight
Giving more than it had
Making invisibles the lead
Splashes of the ocean makes motion
to swirl in my mother's Jergen's lotion
Stepped back from the reproach
to quickly approach
a clean slate, revealing new palettes
Ravening over eye-catching scarlets
Only a Noel Jones would love
such a critical piece
Don't add, don't decrease
just concur to release
such a giving masterpiece
Not me, can't see
conflicts of news, bruises in agony
Hands of lack can't give a blessing
if I have to take it back
Shoulders press down heavy
Heart, gravel to the ground
Harsh critics scratches from my sound
Straight line, round circle
dot the i's, cross the t's
Straight line, round circle
dot the i's, cross the t's
Obsession with perfection
moves me in a session

at the mental institution
Shadowing my way
It's just a perception
Rescue me, from the scenes
of being a perfectionist
24 hours being serious
Can't applaud, no ending never captured it
Finish, I'll never know it
Beyond my limits is in order
Breaking the chains for a do over
Speeding to the Peniel place
Change my name too, as long as I can get
face to face, to state my case
Leary from the tons of dead flesh spreading
God, I need your help down here
Lord I'm begging
Rush me to equanimity
building my black concrete bones
to rest on ability
Pressing the walls of boldness
initiating confidence
demonstrating brilliance
Example my life a struggle through
not a struggle stand still
But still, I got to keep it real
Complicated yes
Simple no
Every earthly being will be put to the test
Relying on the inner being
of my inner being
not from the craziness
of this world, I am seeing
Relaxed emotion can now meditate
to a celebrating completion
build on faith

The Visit

I felt as if I just got a visit from death
My being released from me
No longer was I in control emotionally
Couldn't believe the things
I did or did not say
How I did things a certain way
I reached a total point
in my moment
After being stretched, tugged and bent
I surrender my thoughts, my action, my voice
because to die
was the purpose of the visit
of course
Complete submission I was in
I was out of my way
so I could bend
I now knew humble
and because it took a few
life's happenings to crumble
Light was able to arrive
The visit of eviction force me to survive
showed me who I am to my face
with the outpouring
of His wonderful grace

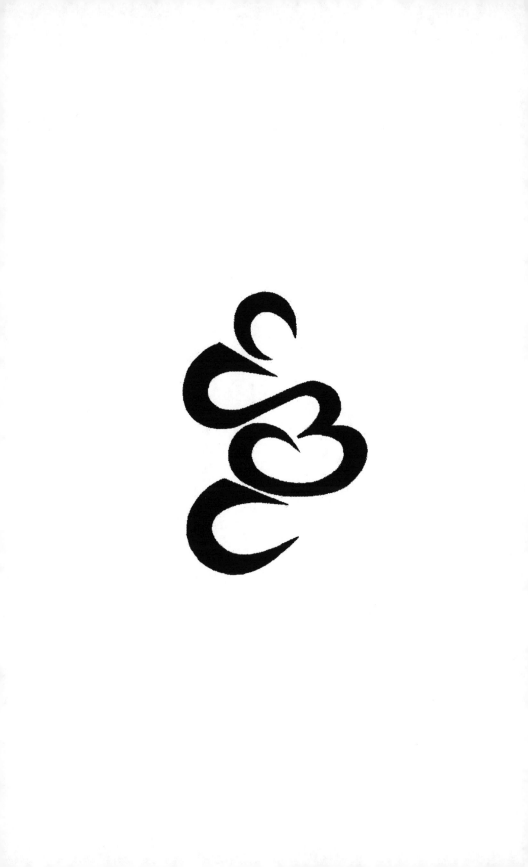

"The Prayer"

Close feelings

I want to follow your will
follow your way
become more like you
everyday
I want you to make me bold
make me strong
hanging with you sometimes
or all day long
I want to know why I am here
why you made me
find out why walking with you
will make my life easy
I want to find a way
to demonstrate love
as you do on this earth
from your throne above
I want to be close with you
as the Father
the Holy Spirit
and the Son
you with me
I with you
becoming the body
as One

REJOICE

Reaching for you, Lord Jesus Christ
Expecting your blessing, you paid the price
Joining in with your Word and loving you
Offering up myself to walk in Your spirit of truth
Interceding for others in need
Connect with Your power to destroy every bad seed
Exalt in your Great name because I have a choice
I know I can live for you and
REJOICE

"Can you please"

I find my nights
Talking to you more
Cause my heart-felt pain
Has my mind sore
Can you please
Remove this
from me right away
So I can make it through
My working day
Can you please
Show the path
you have for me
So I can fulfill your agenda
For my destiny
Can you please
help me get it right
So I can have a peaceful
Sleep at night

Can you please

(extended version)

I find my nights
talking to you more
Cause my heart-felt pain
has my mind sore
Can you please
remove this
from me right away
Whatever you say
I'll do it your way
So I can make it through
my working day
Can you please
show the path
you have for me
Don't let me be
I want to see
So I can fulfill your agenda
for my destiny
Can you please
help me get it right
help me with this fight
standing on your might
so I can have a peaceful
sleep at night

Blessed

Am I living
my life in fear
Of my situation
Knowing that I shouldn't
Cause the Lord
Is my salvation
I will not fear man
My God is in command
I will stand
as I wait on the Lord
Fight off the devil
with my
Lord sword
His Word is near
for me to
Swallow and digest
Releasing it
from my being
I shall be blessed

Thankful

You open my eyes to the rising sun
to let your presents be known
My ears can't help
but hear the beauty
chirping melody from your birds song
I clap along to keep a beat
Cause I know
your present is near
Closer and closer
I feel you reach me
with a sign of joy, from my eye
Fall a happy tear
My feet get to stepping
like someone else
is in control
Your presents in me
makes me feel good
Knowing you're a winner of the soul
My mouth get to mumbling
words fly out before I knew
Lord, I thank you for all you have
given me to express my love to you

It's Me

Do you have a minute
to hear me out
It's me
you know the one
You brought about
I been doing pretty good
on my own
Even though my mom help me
as a child to my teens
but now I'm grown
I know I haven't came
to you many times
Well, not at all
But it's me
the one you knew would desperately
Need you to make the call
The truth is I could use your help
Pressured with the issues
on the surface
Running out of time has me nervous
Can you coach me on what to do
It's me, the one sitting in the church
every other Sunday on the back pew
I need a Word in my spirit
Not a right now Word
for my right now craving
I need a Word to sink into my bones
to cause a radical behaving
It's me
the one who finally went to the alter
and got baptized in the water

Folks telling me
Be careful
watch out for the enemy
I thought I got saved
to fix the inner me
In you I believe there is no lack
it's me
you know the one
who decided to come on back

The Whisper

Still I laid
from the days
radical moving
Restless
from the absences
of my spirit grooving
Faded to a halt
My mind is locked up
in a wicked vault
I can barely hear
the calming whisper
Caught up in wild life
adventure
Stop me, from me
the drama of pollution
The whisper softly
leaks out a solution
Afraid of the silence
thinking your next move
to make my next move
generates in my brain
I'm clicking . . . . ticking
so close to going insane
But the whisper . . . .
if I could just stop
and hear the whisper
Perhaps
I could grab hold
of my future
The whisper
is what settle me

The whisper
protects my vision
when I can't see
The whisper
gently takes
me out of myself
So I can breathe
The whisper
fixes my heart
So I can once again
believe

Love

Love is peace, thoughtful
and kind
And some of us think
its hard to find
Love is to give and forgive
And experience lots
of happiness as we live
Love is to encourage
and be true
Do not be afraid
to express the real you
Love is to be understanding
It makes us grow
Support and motivate
not just those we know
Love needs to be like a world
wide disease with no cure
Love need to
concur the mind
of all mankind
and make our hearts pure

Jesus kind of stuff

Jumping down
Wrestling to stop
For the first round
Got to get to it
Got to get busy
On some
Jesus kind of stuff
Falling is explosive
Getting to the end
Running makes it intensive
Got to look ahead
On some
Jesus kind of stuff
Searching
in the bottles of wine
Tired of bumping walls
not cool walking blind
Got to know for show
calling the unseen bluff
Anxious to dwell among some
Jesus kind of stuff

Special

I came from
the beauty of birth
I saw this mysterious
place call earth
I grew from
day to year
I develop to
function clear
I practice worship
over being religious
I learn from
my imperfections
I draw near
to good direction
I hold fast
to my faith
I know the reward
will be all things great
I follow not
in the flesh
I live Gods laws
for He know best
I exercise the right
to do my part
I intercede for
those laid upon my heart
I hurt for
who know not His name
I pray they know
Him with no shame
I stand on Gods
Word to survive
I die daily
to keep Him alive